Who killed the rule of law?

I0446801

By

R.C.Chavan,

Former Judge, Bombay High Court.

Who killed the rule of law?

A funeral procession was passing through the main streets of the capital. Pallbearers were a black-robed big wig, a white khadi-clad politician just out of jail on parole or furlough for this very purpose, an encounter specialist in khaki, raising his gun occasionally and firing in the air, and a priest cum Bahubali. Mourners as well as pallbearers were jovial, rather boisterously jovial, for they were carrying the body of Rule of law. With great effort, they got rid of the pesky fellow. A provisional death certificate was issued in Ankush Shinde's case, but now came the final death certificate in the Nithari killings. Some asked pallbearers to quicken the step so that after the disposal of the body they had to attend to their routines of protecting their empires. The road ahead branched into two. One leading to a cremation ground and the other to a graveyard. By dint of habit, a dispute broke out about which path to choose. But it was resolved with unusual speed by the flowing black robe, who asked the priest robe if he considered the Rule of law a son of the soil. Prompt came the reply, "No. Certainly NOT." "Then obviously we proceed to the graveyard.," proclaimed the black robe. Khadi and Khaki nodded in agreement, "Let us move fast. Otherwise, some foolish activists will rush and revive the Rule of law as Rajnikant did in Shivaji."

Once in the graveyard, all the mourners rushed carrying shovels to dig a grave, as a priest prepared to commence burial service. They dug a pit that could accommodate not only the Rule of law but pallbearers too, and someone remarked let us push them too. But in all this commotion no one noticed that the body threw the shroud, pushed the priest, and declared that it would read its own obituary and ran away. And this is what fell in the author's lap as the wind from the graveyard blew towards Raj Ghat.

Preface

After reading "Yes My lord, it's you in the mirror", a well-wisher remarked, "The system gave you all the respect and prestige. Why did you wash the dirty linen in public?" Instead of responding, let me append a handful of excerpts of many declamations of the judges and chief justices of the Supreme Court that would summarise the rationale behind writing the book, which incidentally showed only one character in dark hues, with several other judges and lawyers shining with exemplary performance. So it was not washing the dirty linen in public.

In 2015 in the Journal of National Judicial Academy, Justice Raveendran, judge of the Supreme Court writes: *"The number of cases pending in Indian Courts is about 27 million in trial Courts. About 4.5 million before State High Courts and about 70,000 before the Supreme Court. This means an average caseload of 2000 cases per judge. ...After independence, for several years, the number of civil cases and number of criminal cases pending in courts were of equal proportion. Gradually, the proportion of criminal cases has increased. At present, out of the 27.5 million cases pending in trial courts in the country, only about 83 lakhs are civil cases and 192 lakhs are criminal cases, that is, a ratio of 2:5. ...Consequently, there is a real danger of confidence in rule of law and the existing justice delivery system, getting eroded. As a result, people with grievances, causes of action, and complaints start thinking of solutions outside the legal framework to get quick relief. A landlord who wants possession from a tenant, knowing that litigation may take years, starts thinking of engaging the services of musclemen to evict the tenant. More and more reports are received about citizens approaching the underworld or unscrupulous police officers to settle claims and recover properties. Moneylenders, even Banks, instead of approaching Law Courts, have started entrusting debt collection to dubious agencies, who coerce, threaten and bully borrowers to repay the amounts due. Though well aware that such methods are illegal, costly and risky. more and more persons are misled into believing that recourse to illegal methods will give swift, decisive and effective results. In this process. society gets criminalized. This is the most dangerous among the several fallouts of delay.*

The injustice caused on account of delay in criminal cases also requires to be noticed. At any given point of time, there are about three lakh under-trials in prisons, which is about two-third of the prison population. In some States like Bihar, nearly 80% to 85% of the prison population is made up of under-trials. Only in a few states, the percentage of under-trials in prisons is around 50%. More than three thousand under-trials are rotting in jails for more than five years. There are nearly two thousand children behind bars as their mothers are under-trial prisoners. Empirical studies show at least 50% of the under-trials in jail are acquitted on completion of trial. When the under-trials who are behind bars for two or three or four or five years and thereafter acquitted, he or she has no remedy for the years lost, freedom lost, reputation lost. Same is the position for convicted accused, who continue in jails during the pendency of their appeals, hearing of which may take anywhere between one to two years, and even 20 to 25 years in some states."[1]

The same sentiment was echoed by the Supreme Court in Yashpal Jain vs Sushila Devi and others[2] by expressing thus - " *This is a classic case and a mirror to the fact that litigant public may become disillusioned with judicial processes due to inordinate delay in the legal proceedings, not reaching its logical end, and moving at a snail's pace due to dilatory tactics adopted by one or the other party....*

18. Case papers on hand would disclose that dispute between the parties relates back to 02.02.1982 the date of institution of the suit No.2/1982 by the original plaintiff Smt. Urmila Devi. As to the stage of the suit namely, as to whether trial has commenced or otherwise the material available before this court are silent but the fact remains that proceedings have got protracted from 1982 till demise of Urmila Devi on 18.05.2007 and thereafter it has

1   NJA Journal 2015, pp92-112.
2   2023 INSC948

moved at a snail's pace or in other words, the litigation seems to have not been taken to its logical end for reasons best known. ..."

Ankush Maruti Shinde with five others and the accused in Nithari killings cases were saved from certain judicial murders after being incarcerated for over a decade. How did the system fail? The pages to follow are the post mortem notes of 'Rule of law', and an attempt to pen a final cause of its death certificate.

Justice S.B.Sinha, then sitting judge of the Supreme Court, in the same issue of the journal observes: *"Shall we not take seriously the allegation. made by a former President of India. Dr. A.P.J. Abdul Kalam that the criminal justice system in India is about punishing or sending to gallows only the poor? Is Judiciary not responsible for subverting rule of law, not having been able to understand and deal with its problems of delays and arrears? ... Most of the questions raised above, undoubtedly are rather uncomfortable questions? Nobody can deny* **a beginning has to be made, to at least raise these questions** *and what place more befitting for the purpose than this august institution- the National Judicial Academy. ... While the legislature is expected to promulgate laws, the judiciary, as we all know, also has to contribute significantly in the development of law and making law more clear? Are Our Higher Courts really contributing in this direction? ... Can the references be kept pending for many years* *and at times decades altogether?"*[3] But the beginning is still not in sight.

A report in the Times of India dated 11th October, 2023 shows that it took the Supreme Court eight years after Justice Sinha wrote to notice references pending for decades. The report reads that Dr. Justice Chandrachud has decided to 'dust out' 250 (two hundred and fifty) matters; some of them pertaining to sensitive issues referred either to seven or nine judge benches and pending for decades. Obviously, hundreds of more matters may be pending awaiting decisions on these important questions. That the CJI had to 'dust out' 250 references to larger benches pending for decades speaks volumes about the apathy of those who are supposed to lead the judiciary.

Justice Sinha goes on to observe in the same article, *"Does our Supreme Court speak in one, coherent voice? Can we have 25, 26, 27 Supreme Courts in India? Can we have different benches of the same High Court taking extremely conflicting positions on questions of law, which are of national importance? Doesn't the development of law, imparting clarity to law require the judiciary to function as an institution?"*[4]

In the same issue of the journal, Arun Shourie writes, *" Secondly, nothing remains hidden. ... Attitude must be that we are*

3   Ibid pp 77 onwards
4   Ibid.

treating a tumour, because the tumour otherwise will eat the entire institution."[5] This was in the year 2015, in an authoritative journal, and so must have been noticed by the authorities.

Since 2015 till Justice Gogoi took over we have had four Chief Justices. Former Chief Justice of India and honourable member of parliament, Shri Ranjan Gogoi had to say this about the system at an India Today Conclave East: "If you go to court, you don't get a verdict, all you do is wash your dirty linen".[6] He also said that the judiciary in India is in a "ram-shackled" state. This verdict comes after his retirement. Obviously, during his tenure, he could not remedy the ills identified six years ago. Three more chief justices came and went before the fiftieth, the present CJI took over in 2022.

The present Chief Justice of India, Dr. Justice D.Y.Chandrachud said, *"We are aware that the courts in India are extremely burdened, desperately congested. Both literally and metaphorically. According to the study done by PRS Legislative Research, the pendency across all the courts grew by 2.8 per cent annually between 2010 and 2020."*[7] He added that the data available indicates that there are more than 4.1 crore cases pending in district and taluka courts and approximately 59 lakh

5   NJA Journal 2015, pp.150, 151.
6   Scroll 13.02.2021
7   CJI Chandrachud in ILS 19.08.2023

cases are pending in different high courts, with about 71,000 cases pending before the Supreme Court.

This being the official state of affairs, it is better to question those who tore, soiled and splintered the sacred robes and turned them into dirty linen. It is only when I felt that my 'Cries'[8] and 'More Cries'[9] (most of them when I was still in service) fell on deaf ears, did I choose to pen a fictional story to tickle the sleeping beauty- judiciary- to wake it up. But with reactions indicating that at least some still feel that following the path of Gandhiji's three monkeys is the best thing that they can do, the urge to pen this became imperative.

8   Cries in Wilderness' published in 2015
9   More Cries in wilderness Published in 2020.

1. Best of excuses do not change the results.

The authorities knew that there was something seriously wrong with the system. They carried the constitutional responsibility to ensure that the system worked, yet gave excuses. The Supreme Court never denied that the performance of trial courts, or its infrastructure and manpower was also its baby. In fact, it took upon itself a task which was basically the responsibility of the High Courts. (Was it because the apex court perceived that their own selectees in the high courts were not equipped to undertake the work?) Did the world's most powerful Supreme Court lack the power to change the judicial scenario? Or, was this not a priority for it, or did it lack the will? Or, worst still, was the effort restricted to making a show that something was being done?

A popular and frequent refrain is overcrowded, overburdened courts. Fortunately now that the present CJI has not only opened up the entire data, but also decreed that court proceedings will be live streamed, the bluff of overburdened judges will be blown off. The Supreme Court has to just open up data of all courts for scrutiny by academicians, management experts and IT professionals. The myth of huge pendency will be blown off. Attempts to rationalise case types, deciding what qualifies to be a 'case' for statistical purposes are thwarted. A painstakingly prepared report by a committee headed by Justice Bindal is possibly gathering dust in the archives of the court. The fact that our courts are inefficiently run will be visible to everyone once the data is made available by appropriate APIs (Application programme interface). See what researchers have said about the performance of the Supreme Court itself in recently published, "Court on Trial".[10]

In fact, long ago, a documentary was filmed about matters in a court at Badaun UP, titled 'All rise for Your Honour'. Though it was an eye opener, the sacred robes stole the blind fold from the Goddess of Justice and donned on their eyes. In order to show that our courts are overburdened, reference is repeatedly made to judge population ratio. It is compared with the judge population ratio of the United States, where there are 150 judges per million population (in all about 49500 judges) as compared to about 14 judges per million population (about 18200 judges) in India. This is said to be the cause for pendency, delays and all other evils. Statistics can be misleading. What is so sacrosanct about the judge population ratio? Let us find out what is the ratio of litigation (number of cases) to population. As per figures available on the internet, there are about 100.4 million cases 'filed' per year by a population of 330 million, or almost 0.3 cases

10   Court on Trial by Aparna Chandra, Sital Kalantry and William Hubbard.

12

per person. What is this ratio in India with a population of 130 crores (or 1300 millions) and 2.2 crores (22 million) cases 'filed' last year? It is 0.0169 cases per person, or one seventeenth of the cases filed by US citizens. So how is the judge population ratio relevant?

True, that the legislature and the executive do not carry out impact assessment when new laws are enacted to ascertain what additional burden will be thrown on the courts. Without doubt, they ought to do so. The most frequently hurled excuse is lack of executive support in strengthening infrastructure and manpower. But this smear would have stuck to the executive and the legislature had the judiciary shown that it has utilised all available resources fully. Who is responsible for inadequacies in manpower and infrastructure? What is the reality? The truth is that though huge funds were allocated for judicial infrastructure a large portion was left unutilised by the judiciary. Even the grants for phase II of the e-courts project were not fully utilized. The executive or the legislatures could not have obstructed the judiciary's efforts, because ultimately such obstructions could have been judicially removed. It is not that courts have never taken the litigation route to sort out problems with the executive. And a recent stance of a Union government law officer before a bench presided over by Dr. Justice Chandrachud calls off the bluff. It is pointed out that a startling. Rs. 870.71 crores is the unspent central share lying with States and UTs for judicial infrastructure. There are 5193 vacancies in district and subordinate courts out of sanctioned strength of 24485, reducing the working strength to 19292 for whom 20595 court halls are available! Out of the working strength of 17020 only 15391 Judicial Officers are presiding over courts. 531 officers are working in registries.

Justice Raveendran suggests, *"Avoid, or at least reduce drastically, deputing or posting judges to non-judicial/non-adjudicatory work. Liberate judges from Legal Services, in particular organizing and conducting legal awareness programmes and Lok Adalats."*[11] He adds, *"I may also refer to another collateral fallout. Normally, in relation to their judicial functions, judges are not entrusted with any funds for expenditure nor required to submit accounts. With the entrustment of duties relating to Legal Services. huge amounts running into crores of Rupees are being entrusted to Judges, which are required to be spent for providing infrastructure for legal services and for organising legal service events. This has given rise to corruption and indiscriminate spending. Judges should be free from such responsibilities."*[12] But who cares? While we talk of professional managers manning registries, we never fail to add judicial officers to registries. It is said that this is done because they help in

11   Ibid, p.103
12   Ibid p.112

combating corruption in registries. Has corruption in registries come down? Or, is it that judicial officers are posted because they are compliant and trustworthy as their careers are at stake?

Why can the vacancies not be filled up? Because we never bother to go to the root of the problem in finding good talent for judicial service. We start in fits and stop in fits. Merely advertising posts and then somehow recruiting whosoever can prove that he/she has not passed LL.B. examination by cheating by reducing standards, in blatant disregard of any attempt to find out if the candidates possess the qualities required of a judge, amounts, in my humble opinion, an eyewash. Again all aspects of shortcomings in human resource management in judiciary, were brought to the notice of authorities.[13] Need of a National Judicial College or at least courses in National Law Universities to produce quality recruits for the entry level of judicial service was also pressed, agreed upon by authorities but never implemented. No wonder the Supreme Court is flooded with matters which should have been resolved in the courts of the first instance. And my unjustifiable observation is that a trial judiciary lacking essential qualities for judgeship ensures that similar or more glaring lack in the higher courts goes unnoticed, though some sad examples can be found in chapters to follow.

13   'What is wrong with court management? Almost everything!' More
      Cries in Wilderness, p.25

2. Punching bag: bad archaic laws preventing speedy disposal.

For a system obsessed with numbers, disposal, not deciding a case, not doing justice, is the first concern. The Judiciary loves numbers. They help in fooling themselves and people of India in believing how they work under tremendous pressure. Those who never worked or practised in the trial courts and possibly never bothered to even carefully read the procedural codes lambast at the codes. Now there is an additional argument: British era laws, symbols of slavery, forgetting that the Harford Oxbridge gang never fails to follow British and US Courts even now. Though the usual refrain is that our Constitution is the only yardstick to decide cases, judgments are replete with quotes from US and UK courts and Harford Oxbridge sources. When you do not want to use the available tools for speedy and effective delivery of justice, you have no right to tell others what they should be doing. But this is routinely done by all and sundry, just to shirk the responsibility of running this system efficiently.

Since Justice Raveendran had written about declining civil litigation, let me first submit my argument that there is nothing in the Civil Procedure Code which hinders expeditious trials. But lazy logs do not want to read the provisions and do not want to use them. They have a general lament that the procedural laws are bad, without identifying which provision leads to delays. In the scheme of the Civil Procedure Code every provision is aimed at ensuring that points of dispute are duly identified and time of actual trial is reduced. But we encourage flouting those provisions by decrying that rules of procedure are handmaids of justice and can be ignored.[14] The result is that the procedural code is reduced to a dead letter in practice.

Recently, in Yashpal Jain vs Sushila Devi and others,[15] the Supreme Court observed, *"DELAY ON ACCOUNT OF PROCEDURAL LAWS*

27. At the outset, it is necessary to point out the reasons for delay in civil trial namely:
(i) Absence of strict compliance with the provisions of CPC;
(ii) Misuse of processes of the court;
(iii) Lengthy/prolix evidence and arguments. Non-utilization of provisions of the CPC namely
Order X (examination of parties at the first hearing);
(v) Non-Awarding of realistic cost for frivolous and vexatious litigation;
(vi) Lack of adequate training and appropriate orientation course to judicial officers and
lawyers; ...

29. In-fact, the utilization of the provision of CPC to the hilt would reduce the delays. It is on account of non-application of many provisions of the CPC by the presiding officers of the courts

14   Sambhaji vs Gangabai, civil appeal 6731/2008 decided by Supreme Court on 20.11.2008.
15   2023 INSC 948

is one of the reasons or causes for delay in the proceedings or disputes not reaching to its logical conclusion."

Sections 10,11,12 and 47 of the Code prevent multiplicity of proceedings. Section 30 empowers a court to order discoveries, answer interrogatories, admission of documents and facts, production of documents and summon persons to give evidence or produce documents or material objects, **even of its own motion.** Section 32 empowers a court to even imprison a person for default in obeying court's orders. Section 35 places costs fully in the discretion of the court. In addition section 35A empowers courts to order compensatory costs. Sections 36 to 74 not only provide guidance to the executing court in various situations that may arise, clothe the courts with ample powers to ensure execution of decrees and orders. Section 75 empowering courts to issue commissions include even conducting sale of property, among other things. Section 94 empowers a court to issue a warrant to arrest a defendant, order furnishing security, order attachment of properties, issue injunctions, appoint receivers and make such other interlocutory orders as the court may find just and convenient, if it is so prescribed. These prescriptions can be found in 'Orders and rules'. There are comprehensive provisions for appeals against decrees and orders, revisions, and reviews. These among other things provide that a second appeal lies only if the High Court is satisfied that the case involves a substantial question of law. The Code also enables restitution upon reversal of decrees or orders (s.144), enlargement of time fixed by the Code or court (s.148), saves inherent powers of the court to secure ends of justice and prevent abuse of process of court (s.151), correcting errors (ss.152,153).

The orders and rules prescribe how these powers are to be exercised. Having been a 'CP/TP Judge' as the likes of me are derisively called by writ judges who believe in 'BROAD' principles of justice, I have never found any prescription in rules to be the cause of pendency. On the other hand, delay in trials is directly attributable to failure to follow the rules. These rules provide guidance to parties, the bar and the court about the course to be taken in all possible circumstances. For example, when in doubt as to the person from whom redress is sought, the plaintiff may join two or more defendants. (Order I rule 7). Order II rule 2 requires that the plaintiff must include the whole claim. This ensures that there is no multiplicity. I will only briefly refer to provisions meant for speedy disposal which are routinely overlooked.

Order VI rule 1 requires that pleadings 'shall contain and contain only' concise statements of 'material' facts, but not evidence. This Order elaborately states what must be stated and what cannot be included. Rule 4 and 6 require that particulars of misrepresentation, fraud, breach of trust, wilful default, undue influence, or condition precedent must be given. Rule 5 empowers the court to order further and better particulars should this be necessary, and the much abused rule 17 also provides for amending pleadings. Yet, we have prolix pleadings. Why? Because nobody bothers to read the pleadings when they are filed and no judicial officer knows that rule 16 empowers the court to strike out unnecessary, frivolous pleadings which may delay fair trial. If this is religiously done pleadings will be sleek and trials will be fast.

Order VIII about written statements lays down that denials have to be specific. Consequence of failure to file a pleading leads to a decree and consequence of absence of specific denial is that the plea is deemed to have been admitted. Then we have most potent Order X, reading:

'1. At the first hearing of the suit the Court shall ascertain from each party or his pleader whether he admits or denies such allegations of fact as are made in the plaint or written statement (if any) of the opposite party, and as are not expressly or by necessary implication admitted or denied by the party against whom they are made. The Court shall record such admissions and denials.

2. Oral examination of party, or companion of party— (1) At the first hearing of the suit, the Court—(a) shall, with a view to elucidating matters in controversy in the suit examine orally such

of the parties to the suit appearing in person or present in Court, as it deems fit; and

(b) may orally examine any person, able to answer any material question relating to the suit, by whom any party appearing in person or present in Court or his pleader is accompanied.

(2) At any subsequent hearing, the Court may orally examine any party appearing in person or present in Court, or any person, able to answer any material question relating to the suit, by whom such party or his pleader is accompanied.

(3) The Court may, if it thinks fit, put in the course of an examination under this rule questions suggested by either party.

3. Substance of examination to be written— The substance of the examination shall be reduced to writing by the Judge, and shall form part of the record.

4. Consequence of refusal or inability of pleader to answer— (1) Where the pleader of any party who appears by a pleader or any such person accompanying a pleader as is referred to in rule 2, refuses or is unable to answer any material question relating to the suit which the Court is of opinion that the party whom he represents ought to answer, and is likely to be able to answer if interrogated in person, the Court may postpone the hearing of the suit to a future day and direct that such party shall appear in person on such day.

(2) If such a party fails without a lawful excuse to appear in person on the day so appointed, the Court may pronounce judgment against him, or make such order in relation to the suit as it thinks fit.'

These mandatory provisions having potential to curtail trials are reduced to a dead letter. Rule 1 and 2(a) use the word 'shall'. Do the courts have an excuse to avoid examining parties? Yet, without fear of contradiction I may say that in 99.99% of civil cases this is not done. That this provision is not followed is never noticed by any inspecting parties or ever becomes a part of performance appraisal of the officer. Why? 'Rules of procedure are handmaids of justice'.

Order XI about discovery and inspection and order XII about admissions, that can proficiently curtail trials, are also seldom used. If parties fail to avail these provisions, even the court can. But courts have no time. They have to fulfill quota for lok adalats and mediation. Another victim of 'rules of procedure are handmaids of justice' is order XIII rule 2, which lays down that, ' No documentary evidence in the possession or power of any party which should have been, but has not been produced in accordance with the requirements of rule 1 shall be received at any subsequent stage of the proceedings unless good cause is shown to the satisfaction of the Court for the non-production thereof; and the Court receiving any such evidence shall record the reasons for so doing.' Instead of adhering to this provision, everything is reserved for cross examination of the adversary's witness, and courts merrily gulp it.

Procedure to provide a list of witnesses within 15 days of settlement of issues stating the purpose for which the witness is to be summoned contained in order XVI is salutary, yet such established procedure is diluted by judgments holding that not filing such a list does not matter. Order XVII rule 2 lays down that: (a) When the hearing of the suit has commenced, it shall be continued from day-to-day until all the witnesses in attendance have been examined, unless the Court finds that, for the exceptional reasons to be recorded by it, the adjournment of the hearing beyond the following day is necessary.

(b) no adjournment shall be granted at the request of a party, except where the circumstances are beyond the control of that party.

(c) the fact that the pleader of a party is engaged in another Court, shall not be a ground for adjournment.

(d) where the illness of a pleader or his inability to conduct the case for any reason, other than his being engaged in another Court, is put forward as a ground for adjournment, the Court shall not grant the adjournment unless it is satisfied that the party applying for adjournment could not have engaged another pleader in time.

(e) where a witness is present in Court but a party or his pleader is not present or the party or his pleader, though present in Court, is not ready to examine or cross-examine the witness, the Court may, if it thinks fit, record the statement of the witness and pass such orders as it thinks fit dispensing with the examination-in-chief or cross-examination of the witness, as the case may be, by the party or his pleader not present or not ready as aforesaid.

This rule is followed only in breach, because 'rules of procedure are (after all) handmaids of justice!' Had the procedural rules illustratively discussed above been scrupulously followed, trials would have been faster. There is no evidence to show that their breach encouraged by superior courts has resulted in faster, more organised trials. The system is guilty of brazen breach of express provisions of law making one wonder if courts are the places where law is most often breached.

3. Derailing trials by importing American concepts

Our Harford -Oxbridge followers first call a dog mad, and then shoot it. So, first derail the procedure, ensure that justice is delayed, condemn it, and then import American concepts without as much as blinking an eyelid, far from trying to find out how these rules will work in practice. The first such assault on established procedure was made by permitting the filing of affidavits in lieu of examination in chief. The justification is possibly that in civil cases there is hardly anything to be proved by oral evidence. If that is the case, what is the purpose of filing affidavits? Affidavits repeat the case of the parties, many times word by word. Thus what a witness was expected to state from his memory is brought on record in entirety. This effectively kills the rule in section 142 of the Evidence Act that, "Leading questions must not, if objected to by the adverse party, be asked in an examination-in-chief, or in a re-examination, except with the permission of the Court. The Court shall permit leading questions as to matters which are introductory or undisputed, or which have, in its opinion, been already sufficiently proved."

Section 5 of the Evidence Act mandates that "5. Evidence may be given in any suit or proceeding of the existence or non-existence of every fact in issue and of such other facts as are hereinafter declared to be relevant, **and of no others**." (emphasis supplied). When a witness deposes in a court, either physically or virtually, the questions about admissibility on the ground of relevancy as well as other grounds, will be put and decided then and there as prescribed in section 136, which reads as under: "Judge to decide as to admissibility of evidence. —When either party proposes to give evidence of any fact, the Judge may ask the party proposing to give the evidence in what manner the alleged fact, if proved, would be relevant; and the Judge shall admit the evidence if he thinks that the fact, if proved, would be relevant, and not otherwise.

If the fact proposed to be proved is one of which evidence is admissible only upon proof of some other fact, such last-mentioned fact must be proved before evidence is given of the fact first-mentioned, unless the party undertakes to give proof of such fact, and the Court is satisfied with such undertaking.

If the relevancy of one alleged fact depends upon another alleged fact being first proved, the Judge may, in his discretion, either permit evidence of the first fact to be given before the second fact is proved, or require evidence to be given of the second fact before evidence is given of the first fact."

So first there is a danger of irrelevant evidence being pushed through affidavits. If the examination in chief itself is bulky, the cross examiner will have a field day and the cross examination will be obese. Again those who do not care about procedural safeguards submit that where is the need to sift what is admissible and what is not at that stage? All this can be done at the stage of writing judgment and time of court in hearing objections and ruling on admissibility could be saved. Unfortunately, the Supreme Court has come out with conflicting orders to rule on objections to admissibility. First, in Bipin Shantilal vs State of Gujarat, (2002)10 SCC 529, decided on 22.02.2001, a three-Judge Bench ruled that documents or evidence objected to may be exhibited/recorded tentatively subject to the objection to be decided finally in the judgment. In R.V.E. Venkatachala vs Arulmigu Viswesaraswam, (2003) 8 SCC 752 decided on 08.10.2003 and Shalimar Chemical Works vs Surendra Oil, (2010) 8 SCC 423 decided on 27.08.2010, by two judge benches, procedure of tentatively admitting evidence subject to objection was faulted. This was of course not the last word. In suo motu writ (Crl) no.(s) 1/2017, in re: to issue certain guidelines regarding inadequacies and deficiencies in criminal trials ….petitioner(s) versus the state of Andhra Pradesh & ors. ….respondent(s), a three judge bench headed by the CJI held:

"15. Apart from Section 148, there are other provisions of the Evidence Act (Sections 149-154) which define the ground rules for cross examination. During questioning, no doubt, the counsel for the party seeking cross examination has considerable leeway;

cross examination is not confined to matters in issue, but extends to all relevant facts. However, if the court is not empowered to rule, during the proceeding, whether a line of questioning is relevant, the danger lies in irrelevant, vague and speculative answers entering the record. Further, based on the answers to what (subsequently turn out to be irrelevant, vague or otherwise impermissible questions) more questions might be asked and answered. If this process were to be repeated in case of most witnesses, the record would be cluttered with a jumble of irrelevant details, which at best can be distracting, and at worst, prejudicial to the accused. Therefore, this court is of the opinion that the view in Bipin Shantilal Panchal should not be considered as binding. The presiding officer therefore, should decide objections to questions, during the course of the proceeding, or failing it at the end of the deposition of the concerned witness. This will result in decluttering the record, and, what is more, also have a salutary effect of preventing frivolous objections. In given cases, if the court is of the opinion that repeated objections have been taken, the remedy of costs, depending on the nature of obstruction, and the proclivity of the line of questioning, may be resorted to. Accordingly, the practice mandated in Bipin Shantilal Panchal shall stand modified in the above terms."

Unfortunately the further directions given by the three judge bench to incorporate draft rules for recording evidence annexed to the order does not seem to have been implemented. Can it be said that time of the court will be saved by postponing ruling on admissibility? Once a piece of evidence goes on record, further questions, cross-examination on those pieces of evidence is bound to be there. Rather more time will be lost. And affidavits in lieu of examination in chief have a potential of allowing unchecked entry of a lot of irrelevant and inadmissible material to make matters worse for the judge while preparing judgment.

So keen are the Harford-Oxbridge experts to save time of poor trial judges that they suggest that commissioners should be appointed for recording evidence. If the trial judge is to be presented with an entire dossier prepared by someone else, is not to get a chance to look at the parties and witnesses, cannot observe how a question is put and how the answer is given, what is the difference between a trial court and an appellate court? The so called loss of time in trials about which mostly those who never conducted trials lament, is in fact necessary to enable not only the trial judge, but advocates for both the parties to mentally evaluate the evidence as it is tendered, formulate how the advocates are going to deal with each piece and formulate how the piece is going to be dealt with in the judgment for the trial judge. Since none can switch off minds as all this is unfolding, the process of revising evaluation of each piece of evidence is continuously going on. This is what finally shapes a good judgment. Exceptions of judges mechanically presiding over trials are there, but they should not be ideals which the system permits. Justice fails when you reduce trial court to a court which merely reads dead letters with supersonic speed, chooses 'Yes' or 'No' answers and then searches for reasons from the record. It is for the judicial policy makers to spell out what is their idea of work in trial court and decide if they want to go for inanimate dead trial proceedings, or for deliberative live proceedings.

This is important for the Bar too. Skills of reaching to truth and in any case unmasking lies could be learnt only in live proceedings before a judge presiding over the trial, rather than a commissioner, who would only submit a transcript with a number of objections to rule upon. If we want the Bar as well as judges to improve their skills in unearthing truth, finding out where justice lies, live trials are necessary. Commissioners are to be employed only when it is not possible for a witness to be physically present in the court. But now, with facilities for video conferencing, there is absolutely no need to blindfold the trial judge and make him just hear the transcripts.

Who pays for the commissioner? Of course, the parties. So the scheme is to make the judicial process costlier so that people avoid coming to the courts. ADR is another such import without a thought about realities in our society. First, as far as interpersonal disputes are concerned, the parties do go to elders in the community, many times panchayats, before coming to the court. As for business community and commercial disputes, do our adjudicators not know that every business community has a local association for each type of business, like grain merchants association, cloth merchants association and the like? Aggrieved businessmen first approach such associations, whose members know not only the nitty gritty of the business, but are aware of the market situations, reputation of parties and come up with workable solutions. Only when the problem remains unresolved do the parties approach the courts. Yet, rather than hearing the parties, we choose to push them to ADR, again at a cost. To popularise ADR, High Courts have fixed quotas for cases referred for ADR or lok adalats. Examination of these proceedings will show how we have pushed our trial courts into 'cheating' to fill their ADR quotas and in the process getting obliged by advocates. Disputes already settled are pushed to lok adalats to put a formal stamp of disposal. Since the entire data is available on NJDG, some researcher will surely show us that ADR has neither eased pendency nor injected speed in the system.

It is humbly submitted that pushing litigants to ADR or appointing commissioners for recording evidence is unlikely to make litigants feel that his case was dealt with by a court of law. Instead of considering these shortcuts, let the system invest in strengthening trial courts by a thorough recruitment and training process which will ensure that our trial judges use all available tools to do justice rather than focus on numbers. Bar can also be encouraged to have more efficient litigation lawyers. Once the quality of legal assistance available is raised and more options of efficient advocates become available, with the use of ICT tools the cost of litigation will come down. System will gain momentum. Judicial officers will not be required to induce litigants into choosing alternatives by suggesting to them that litigation is costly and time consuming.

4. Ankush Shinde, Nithari and failure of criminal justice system.

Judgment of Allahabad High Court in Nithari killings setting aside death sentences, the prospect of being hanged at which accused was staring for over a decade was an encore of Ankush Maruti Shinde vs State of Maharashtra. The only silver line was that the High Court itself pointed to faulty investigation, rather than waiting for a review by the Supreme Court of its own judgment sentencing six persons to death. After the judgment in review in Ankush Shinde came, I had written an elaborate article pointing out how useful safeguards and checks in Criminal Procedure Code had been consistently ignored.

It is not that the judiciary was not concerned about all tainted politicians, goons, history sheeter proclaiming from rooftops that they have full faith in our criminal justice system. From time to time the judiciary had examined the problem from their lens and suggested solutions, like separation of prosecution machinery from police, separating crime detection and criminal investigation wing of police from law and order wing, and placing criminal investigation under prosecution wing. There can be no doubt that these well meaning solutions ought to have been implemented, though as a trial magistrate and judge my experience shows that police officers involved in law and order are equally good in investigation. Many experienced and senior police officers have explained why law and order cannot be divorced from criminal investigation. Criminals and breach of law and order are inseparably wedded. As for conducting prosecutions, when magistracy was still with executive, we had 'prosecuting jamadars' (head constables) in magisterial courts, and I personally know of at least three who rose to be excellent district and sessions judges, with one of them being one of the best joint directors of judicial officers training institute.

My approach to any problem is to find out what we can do in the given situation, because expecting other authorities or agencies to take remedial measures amounts first, to passing the buck; secondly, to exhibit our ignorance of available tools at our disposal and our inability to use them; and lastly, forgetting the last phrase in our oath, 'to uphold the constitution and the laws'. This implies that we ensure that provisions of law are not ignored, but fully implemented in our courts, and this is what I have suggested in "Rebuilding confidence in the criminal justice system."

Rather than asking the readers to go to that article, republished in "More Cries in Wilderness"[16], I will quote from the article on how courts have neutralised checks and encouraged

16   Rebuilding Confidence in Criminal Justice system, p.44, "More Cries In Wilderness".

collapse of criminal justice, as also what needs to be done to rebuild confidence in the criminal justice system.

While speaking at Mumbai on the 17th August 2019, Hon. Dr. Justice Chandrachud observed that Court monitored investigations show better results. His lordship highlighted the difficulties that judges face on account of shoddy investigation. Disastrous consequences of heartless investigation leading to filing a half baked charge-sheet came to the fore this year when by a judgment delivered on the 5th March 2019 in criminal appeal nos. 1008-1009 of 2007, Ankush Maruti Shinde and others versus State of Maharashtra, a bench of the Supreme Court set aside the death sentence imposed by the Court itself in 2009 on six convicts and acquitted all of them holding that the investigation was faulty. Thus not only were innocent persons made to stare at death for almost 13 years, the family of the victims was cheated into believing that the perpetrators of ghastly gang rapes and murders had been brought to book. Justice Raveendran observed in his well researched article in NJA Journal, *"The injustice caused on account of delay in criminal cases also requires to be noticed. At any given point of time, there are about three lakh under-trials in prisons, which is about two-third of the prison population. In some States like Bihar, nearly 80% to 85% of the prison* *population is made up of under-trials. Only in a few states, the percentage of under-trials in prisons is around 50%. More than three thousand under-trials are rotting in jails for more than five years. There are nearly two thousand children behind bars as their mothers are under-trial prisoners. Empirical studies show at least 50% of the under-trials in jail are acquitted on completion of trial. When the under-trials who are behind bars for two or three or four or five years and thereafter acquitted, he/she has no remedy for the years lost, freedom lost, reputation lost. Same is the position for convicted accused, who continue in jails during the pendency of their appeals. hearing of which may take anywhere between one to two years, and even 20 to 25 years in some states.*''[17] This could happen only because all the checks provided in the Criminal Procedure Code were ignored.*

Why do cases like Ankush Shinde or Nithari killings happen? Whenever there is any ghastly crime, the police as well as ruling politicians are under a pressure to find miscreants and book them. Unable to find real culprits, police take to picking up scapegoats, cook up evidence and push a half baked chargesheet. Apart from Ankush Shinde and Nithari, let us not forget the celebrated Malegaon bomb blast case, which is still being tried. In that case, a high profile investigating team had duly picked up half a dozen persons who were duly sent for trial with confessions

17   NJA Journal p.99-100.

of some of them on record. Now another group of persons are being tried for the same offence.

The magistrates had received the charge-sheets, but did not believe that they were expected to check the chargesheets because we have turned magistrates into post offices as far as offences triable by court of sessions are concerned. They routinely committed the case to the court of sessions. In Ankush Shinde's case, the sessions judge neither noticed any deficiency in the charge-sheet or police papers, nor paid any heed to the requirement of law that charge could be framed only if the material submitted led to presumption that the accused were guilty. Even after the trial the sessions judge did not find anything amiss, as he held the case was rarest of rare warranting death penalty for six persons. A division bench of the High Court hearing death reference too did not find anything wrong, except that it reduced the death sentence of three of the six persons to life imprisonment. A two judge bench of the Supreme Court allowed the State's appeal and dismissed that of convicts, restoring death sentences to all. The question was about the lives of six persons. Should the common man conclude that one magistrate, one session judge, two judges each of the High Court and the Supreme Court were so careless in their scrutiny of material that they did not notice that innocent persons were being tried? Had the convicts been hanged between this final sentence in 2009 and the review in 2018, what would have happened? Now 16 years after the incident what are the chances of real culprits being brought to book?

Magistracy with judiciary is simply oblivious to the powers and duties of magistrates in investigation. They believe that they embody a blindfolded goddess of justice holding scales. This impression was fortified by stray observations by superior courts advising judicial magistrates to distance themselves from investigation. So investigation provisions in the Code have become a dead letter. That area is no man's land, judiciary not overseeing it because it is believed to be an executive function, and executive magistrates overlooking it as eventually what happens to investigation is judiciary's concern. This gave investigating agencies a free hand with none to guide or correct them. This absence of authority overseeing investigation leads to political interference and scuttled investigation. Considering the disastrous results of this apathy towards bringing real culprits to book, and frequent encroachment on the time of the Apex court, it is necessary to remind the magistracy of its powers and duties in investigations and trials.

There are numerous occasions for a magistrate to monitor an investigation. The Code requires FIR to be sent to the magistrate without delay. It is received, possibly entered into a register and forgotten till a remand application is received.

Ideally, if the FIR did not lead to the filing of any application before the magistrate, after waiting for a week, the magistrate ought to be calling the case diary. This is permissible since an Inquiry is defined in the Code to mean every inquiry, other than a trial, conducted under this Code **by a Magistrate** or Court. [Section 2(g) of the Code] And receipt of the FIR could be taken to be the commencement of Inquiry. Further, section 170(2) of the Code empowers a court conducting an inquiry (or even a trial) to send for case diaries and may use such diaries to aid it in such inquiry (or trial). If this is done, the magistrate will know what steps have been taken by the investigation officer and whether they conform to the standard practice, and prescribed safeguards.

Most potent provision is S.167 CrPC, which too requires a case diary to be sent to the magistrate. While granting or refusing remand, a note by the magistrate about what ought to have been done, or what is overlooked will ensure that investigation is on track. The investigation agency need not fear that there could be leaks when investigation is still going on, because, the Code prescribes that "Neither the accused nor his agents shall be entitled to call for such diaries, nor shall he or they be entitled to see them merely because they are referred to by the Court"; except at trial and subject to several limitations.

On the role of a magistrate in investigation, in Sakiri Vasu v. State of UP (2008) 2 SCC 409, in the following words the

39

Supreme Court clarified that the magistrate's powers in course of investigation are wide:

17. In our opinion Section 156(3) CrPC is wide enough to include all such powers in a Magistrate which are necessary for ensuring a proper investigation, and it includes the power to order registration of an FIR and of ordering a proper investigation if the Magistrate is satisfied that a proper investigation has not been done, or is not being done by the police. Section 156(3) CrPC, though briefly worded, in our opinion, is very wide and it will include all such incidental powers as are necessary for ensuring a proper investigation.

18. It is well settled that when a power is given to an authority to do something it includes such incidental or implied powers which would ensure the proper doing of that thing. In other words, when any power is expressly granted by the statute, there is impliedly included in the grant, even without special mention, every power and every control the denial of which would render the grant itself ineffective. Thus where an Act confers jurisdiction it impliedly also grants the power of doing all such acts or employ such means as are essentially necessary for its execution."

Alas, the Court recognised the power, but did not expressly say that not exercising power vested when needed amounts to abdication of duty. There are laws and laws to ensure that criminal trials are completed efficiently without delay.

Unfortunately there is no law that these laws have to be followed by trial courts unless the Supreme Court or the High courts so direct. And, if these superior courts ever dilute the requirements of provisions mandating speedy and efficient trials, then the trial courts believe that those provisions are erased from the statute book. Just as in the case of provisions for supervising investigations, provisions about speedy trials have also become a dead letter.

The bane of the system is flouting procedural provisions under the specious principle that rules of procedure are handmaids of justice. Exceptions which superior courts often sanctify, simply because the unscrupulous wealthy litigant, or a haughty successful practitioner, who is habituated to lower courts waiting for him or her, takes the trouble of knocking the doors of these superior courts crying "Injustice, My Lord, in the name of procedural rules!" hurt the system. And the 'kind' heart of "My lords" melts on it being made to appear to them that refusal of the trial judge to ignore delay of a year here or there may lead to denial of justice! They feel that with thousands of cases pending for years, the trial court need not be vexed by delays of a few days here or there. Giving the judges of superior courts a benefit of doubt, one may say that they are not made aware that the root cause of delays is the attitude of 'taking time' limits lightly. Timid trial judges, having long forgotten the part of the oath

41

requiring them to do justice without fear, are mortally scared of the wrath of judges in higher courts who can make or mar their careers, and so, many times, even without waiting for Lordship's command they readily derail a trial.

The first step to avoid needless downpour of rubbish on courts is to exercise the power of not issuing process in a half baked charge-sheet, or a criminal complaint. If courts refuse to issue a process when material is deficient the courts would be saving a person from going through the ordeal of engaging a lawyer, furnishing bail, court appearances, etc. The courts would also be de-clogging their cause lists as well as clearing space in their unkempt record rooms. And most importantly, the tendency of the investigating agency to submit any 'rag tag' as 'charge-sheet', would be curbed, and the quality of investigation would improve. Victims will feel secure with real culprits being booked. People at large would also be able to see that an offender could roam free, not because of lapses in the judicial process or much abused advocacy, but due to faulty investigation. Can this be done? Certainly.

In Abhinandan Jha & Ors vs Dinesh Mishra, AIR 1968 SC 117, the Court observed as under:

"We have already referred to s.190, which is the first section in the group of sections headed 'Conditions requisite for Initiation of Proceedings.' Sub-s. (1), of this section, will cover a

report sent, under s. 173. The use of the words 'may take cognizance of any offence', in sub-s. (1) of s. 190 in our opinion imports the exercise of a 'judicial discretion', and the Magistrate, who receives the report, under s. 173, will have to consider the said report and judicially take a decision, whether or not to take cognizance of the offence. From this it follows that it is not as if that the Magistrate is bound to accept the opinion of the police that there is a case for placing the accused on trial. **It is open to the Magistrate to take the view that the facts disclosed in the report do not make out an offence for taking cognizance** *or he may take the view that there is no sufficient evidence to justify an accused being put on trial. On either of these grounds, the Magistrate will be perfectly justified in declining to take cognizance of an offence, irrespective of the opinion of the police."* (emphasis supplied).

What prevents Magistrates from refusing to issue a process on a defective charge-sheet on incomplete investigation? Because this work does not earn any credits, though, this can also be changed. A disposal of such nature could earn credit. In fact, with at most caution, I feel it can earn a greater credit compared to post trial disposal. Because, if the problem is nipped in the bud, all future listings, hearings, orders, appeals, and, of course, the much abused recourse to section 482 of the Code of Criminal Procedure would be avoided. Rather than earning dishonest credit

43

for killing a dead case, magistrates would love to earn credits for quality work that will enhance their judging skills, test their abilities in presiding over highly contested trials and give real purport to their power. Just as High courts have started recognising disposal through mediation, about which the legal fraternity is sceptical, the administration could give credit for charge-sheets -final reports- which are rejected and in which process is not issued. It is important to put a rider here. After reading this suggestion, many would think that this may lead to Magistrates rejecting even genuine charge-sheets for winning credits. This possibility would be very bleak, for rejecting a charge-sheet would require well reasoned order. Needless to say, reasons for rejecting a charge-sheet would have to withstand a far stronger test than reason of mere existence of 'prima facie' case required for issuing a process. With speedier trials, public confidence in the system would increase and more aggrieved persons would take recourse to legal remedies, rather than approach extra constitutional authorities.

But what about the legal fraternity? How would the burgeoning army of advocates (about which Justice Raveendran speaks in his lecture published in the NJA journal) without briefs take it? Would they feel that their opportunity of making a living is cut short? Would some ingenious soul argue that it is infringement of the hallowed fundamental right to life? I think no.

Because, once the legal fraternity knows that rejecting a charge-sheet at the threshold is possible, clients will contact lawyers before the charge-sheet is filed and they would be able to argue that the charge-sheet be rejected, rather than saying that only the High court could quash a charge-sheet. This would rather open up a new channel of work for lawyers as challenges to orders refusing to take cognizance upon a charge-sheet will also be possible.

Another ritual which is ritualistically performed by criminal courts is framing charges, which marks the beginning of trial. Provisions in the Criminal Procedure code about making out a case for framing charges are routinely ignored. The popular belief is that it is always better to hand down an acquittal after trial than discharge the offender, not realising how much does it cost to the exchequer as well as litigant to face a trial, apart from occupying scarce court time. A considerable amount of confusion prevails because of judicial exposition of provisions relating to nature and scope of enquiry contemplated at the stage of framing of charge. The cause of this confusion is reading observations in judgments like provisions in the statute and then going on expanding them. There are two aspects to an enquiry at the stage of framing charge: What is the scope of enquiry at the stage of framing charge and what is the object of that enquiry?

To grasp the context it may be useful to first refer to sections 227, 228, 239, 240, 245, 246 of the Code of Criminal Procedure.

For the sake of analysis, relevant phrases or expressions used in these sections may be tabulated as under:

Type of trial	When can charge be framed	When should the accused be discharged
Sessions Trial	**that there is ground for presuming that the accused has committed an offence (s.228)**	**there is not sufficient ground for proceeding against the accused, (s.227)**
Warrant trial on police report	**that there is ground for presuming that the accused has committed an offence (s.240)**	**considers the charge against the accused to be groundless, he shall discharge the accused, (s.239)**
Warrant trial on private complaint	**that there is ground for presuming that the accused has committed an offence (s.246)**	**that no case against the accused has been made out which, if unrebutted, would warrant his conviction, the Magistrate shall discharge him. (s.245)**

It may thus be seen that as far as framing of charge in all the three types of trials, the standard prescribed is the same, namely, **that there is ground for presuming that the accused**

46

has committed an offence. Plain reading of the provisions does not reflect any ambiguity to justify undertaking an interpretational voyage. Thus, the material before the court should justify drawing a presumption that the accused has committed an offence triable by such court. If such material is not available, what does the court do? If it cannot frame charge, the only other option available is discharge, irrespective of the fact that the legislature has chosen three different expressions in sections 227, 239 and 245, as also the normal principle of statutory interpretation that when legislature uses different expressions, it has different intent. Though different expressions are used, if carefully considered, it would be clear that the same result is intended. What is meant by **"there is not sufficient ground for proceeding against the accused,"**? Would the sessions court proceed if it finds that the case is surely to end in acquittal, even if material tendered by the prosecution is taken as it is for its face value? Obviously not. The expression used in s.239 also points to a similar requirement: if the charge is groundless, why should a court undertake a farcical trial? The expression in section 245 is more accentuated. It requires, **"that no case against the accused has been made out which, if unrebutted, would warrant his conviction,"** for discharging the accused. This is because unlike the earlier two types of trial, the court does not just have a police report and material collected by police during investigation. In this trial

47

actual evidence has been recorded by the trial court. But this too is consistent corollary to the requirement of framing charge, namely, that there must be ground for **presuming** that the accused has committed an offence. For, the question of rebuttal would arise only if there is a presumption. So the minimum that is clearly deducible from these provisions is that if the court finds that the material before it, even if accepted as true, is insufficient for handing down a conviction, the accused ought to be discharged.

It may now be useful to note how the Supreme Court has looked at these requirements. In Century Spinning vs State Of Maharashtra decided on 13 October, 1971, reported in AIR 1972 SC 545, 1972 CriLJ 329, a three judge bench of the Supreme court was called upon to decide the interrelation of the provisions relating to framing of charge and discharge in section 251A of the old CrPC, which are same as in the new Code in form of sections 239 and 240. In that case the magistrate had discharged the accused and the prosecution took the matter to the High Court, which ordered framing of charge. In this context, after considering the rival contentions, while setting aside the order of the High Court and restoring that of the magistrate, the Supreme court observed as under:

"Though at the bar of this Court as also in the High Court considerable arguments and discussion centred round this point,

*in our opinion, the construction and meaning of this section so far as relevant for our purpose does not present any difficulty. Under Sub-section (2), if upon consideration of all the documents referred to in Section 173, Criminal P.C. and examining the accused, if considered necessary by the Magistrate and also after hearing both sides, the Magistrate considers the charge to be groundless, he must discharge the accused. This subsection has to be read along with Sub-section (3), according to which, if after considering the documents and hearing the accused, the Magistrate thinks that there is ground for presuming that the accused has committed an offence triable under Chapter XXI of the Code with in the Magistrate's competence and for which he can punish adequately, he has to frame in writing a charge against the accused. **Reading the two sub-sections together it clearly means that if there is no ground for presuming that the accused has committed an offence, the charges must be considered to be groundless, which is the same thing as saving that there is no ground for framing the charges.** This necessarily depends on the facts and circumstances of each case and the Magistrate is entitled and indeed has a duty to consider the entire material referred to in Sub-section (2). On the view that we have taken, we do not consider it necessary to refer to the various decided cases cited at the bar of this Court or discussed in the judgment of the High Court.*

*16. ... **The argument that the Court at the stage of framing the charges has not to apply its judicial mind for considering whether or not there is a ground for presuming the commission of the offence by the accused is not supportable either on the plain language of the section or on its judicial interpretation or on any other recognised principle of law. The order framing the charges does substantially affect the person's liberty and it is not possible to countenance the view that the Court must automatically frame the charge merely because the prosecuting authorities, by relying on the documents referred to in Section 173, consider it proper to institute the case.** The responsibility of framing the charges is that of the Court and it, has to judicially consider the question of doing so. Without fully adverting to the material on the record it must not blindly adopt the decision of the prosecution.*" (emphasis supplied)

I have not come across any judgement of the Supreme Court coming from a bench of higher strength disapproving these observations.

Some digression seems to have originated from the judgment in **State Of Bihar vs Ramesh Singh reported at** AIR 1977 SC 2018, 1978 SCR (1) 257. In that case, an Additional Sessions Judge accepted the plea of the accused and discharged the accused. The State went in revision before the High Court to assail the aforesaid order of the Sessions Court. The High Court dismissed the revision. When the matter reached the Supreme Court, the Court held, *"... **But at the initial stage if** there is a strong suspicion which leads the Court to think that **there is ground for presuming that the accused has committed an offence then it is not open to the Court to say that there is no sufficient ground for proceeding against the accused.** The presumption of the guilt of the accused which is to be drawn at the initial stage is not in the sense of the law governing the trial of criminal cases in France where the accused is presumed to be guilty unless the contrary is proved. But it is only for the purpose of deciding prima facie whether the Court should proceed with the trial or not. **If the evidence which the Prosecutor proposes to adduce to prove the guilt of the accused even if fully accepted before it is challenged in cross-examination or rebutted by the defence evidence, if any, cannot show that the accused committed the offence, then there will be no sufficient ground for proceeding with the trial**. ... In Nirmaljit Singh Hoon v. The State of West Bengal and another Shelat, J. delivering the judgment on behalf of the majority for the Court referred at page 79 of the report to the earlier decisions of this Court in Chandra Deo Singh v. Prakash Chandra Bose **where this Court was held to have laid down with reference to the similar provisions contained in sections 202 and 203 of the Code of Criminal Procedure**, 1898 "that the test was whether there was sufficient* *ground for proceeding and not whether there was sufficient ground for conviction, and observed that where there was prima facie evidence, even though the person charged of an offence in the complaint might have a defence, the matter had to be left to be decided by the appropriate forum at the appropriate stage and issue of a process could not be refused." Illustratively, Shelat J, further added "Unless, therefore, the Magistrate finds that the evidence led before him is self-contradictory, or intrinsically untrustworthy, process cannot be refused if that evidence makes out a prima facie case."* (emphasis supplied).

It is humbly submitted that the cause of all further misunderstanding and deviation about the law as to framing charge or discharging the accused is the unfortunate observation in Ramesh Singh that the provisions contained in sections 202 and 203 of the Code of Criminal Procedure, 1898 were similar to those laying down requirements for framing charge or discharging the accused. Even after noticing that the observations in Nirmaljit Singh Hoon and Chandra Dev Singh came in the context of scrutiny at the stage of issuing process, in Ramesh Singh the court chose to apply that standard for deciding whether a person was to be charged or not. The Court ought to have realised that at the stage of issuing process, the accused is not at all in the picture. The first opportunity that the accused gets to address the court is at the stage of framing charge. If the same standard, as is applicable at the stage of issuing process is to be applied for framing charge, there was no need to provide for this stage and needlessly waste time, since if by applying one standard the magistrate has already come to some conclusion, by applying the same standard again to the same material, the magistrate may not be expected to come to different conclusion. This deviation in Ramesh Singh was without even referring to the apt observations in Century Spg. & Mfg. Co., which were directly on the question of level of scrutiny at the stage of framing charge. Therefore, the judgment in Ramesh Singh, rendered in ignorance of judgment in Century Spg & Mfg Co., it is humbly submitted, must be held to be *per incuriam*.

Consequently, the judgment in Union Of India vs Prafulla Kumar Samal & Anr. reported at AIR 1979 SC 366, 1979 SCR (2) 229, relying on the observations in Ramesh Singh, too need not be read as diluting the observations in Century.

After considering these observations, in Satish Mehra v. Delhi Administration and Another [(1996) 9 SCC 766], the Court held as under:

"At this stage it is superfluous to consider whether the FIR is liable to be quashed as both sides argued on the sustainability of the charge framed by the Sessions Judge. We are, therefore, considering the main question whether the Sessions Court should have framed the charge against the appellant as it did

53

now. ...When those two sections are put in juxtaposition with each other the test to be adopted becomes discernible: Is there sufficient ground for proceeding against the accused? It is axiomatic that the standard of proof normally adhered to at the final stage is not to be applied at the stage where the scope of consideration is where there is "sufficient ground for proceeding". (Vide State of Bihar v. Ramesh Singh, AIR 1977 SO 2018, and Supdt, & Remembrancer of Legal Affairs, West Bengal v. Anil Kumar Bhunja, 1979 Cr. L.J. 1390: AIR 1980 SC 52).

... At the same time the Court cautioned that a roving enquiry into the pros and cons of the case by weighing the evidence as if he was conducting the trial is not expected or even warranted at this stage."

The court then referred to, *"An incidental question which emerges in this context is whether the Session Judge can look into any material other than those produced by the prosecution. Section 226 of the Code obliges the prosecution to describe the charge brought against the accused and to state by what evidence the guilt of the accused would be proved. The next provision enjoins on the Session Judge to decide whether there is sufficient ground to proceed against the accused. In so deciding the Judge has to consider (1) the record of the case and (2) the documents produced therewith. He has then to hear the submissions of the accused as well as the prosecution on the limited question whether there is sufficient ground to proceed. What is the scope of hearing the submissions? Should it be confined to hearing oral arguments alone?"*

The Court added, *"Similar situations arise under Section 239 of the Code (which deals with trial of warrant cases on police reports). In that situation the Magistrate has to afford the prosecution and the accused an opportunity of being heard besides considering the police report and the documents sent therewith. At this stage the Code enjoins on the Court to give audience to the accused for deciding whether it is necessary to proceed to the next stage. It is a matter of exercise of judicial mind. There is nothing in the code which shrinks the scope of such audience to oral arguments. If the accused succeeds in producing any reliable material at that stage which might fatally affect even the very sustainability of the case, it is unjust to suggest that no such material shall be looked into by the Court at that stage. Here the "ground" may be any valid ground including insufficiency of evidence to prove charge.*

The object of providing such an opportunity as is envisaged in Section 227 of the code is to enable the Court to decide whether it is necessary to proceed to conduct the trial. If the case ends there it gains a lot of time of the Court and saves much human effort and cost. If the materials produced by the accused even at that early stage would clinch the issue, why should the Court shut it out saying that such documents need be produced only after wasting a lot more time in the name of trial proceedings. Hence, we are of the view that the Sessions Judge would be within his powers to consider even material which the accused may produce at the stage contemplated in Section 227 of the Code.

But when the Judge is fairly certain that there is no prospect of the case ending in conviction the valuable time of the Court should not be wasted for holding a trial only for the purpose of formally completing the procedure to pronounce the conclusion on a future date. We are under heavy pressure of work-load. If the Sessions Judge is almost certain that the trial would only be an exercise in futility or a sheer waste of time it is advisable to truncate or ship(sic sink?) the proceedings at the stage of Section 227 of the Code itself." (emphasis supplied).

It may be noted that on the main question about standard of scrutiny at the stage of framing of charge, the even after considering Ramesh Singh and Prafull Kumar, the Court held that it is advisable to truncate or drop the proceedings at the stage of Section 227 of the Code itself. There was no doubt about the conclusion that a judge may not charge an accused if he is fairly certain that the trial is to end in an acquittal. The observations on incidental question, namely that even material produced by the accused could be looked into, led a two judge bench in Debendra

Nath Padhi to doubt the correctness of these observations and the bench made a reference to a larger bench.

On these further observations, a larger three judge bench in State Of Orissa vs Debendra Nath Padhi (AIR 2005 Supreme Court 359) formulated the following question for consideration:

"Can the trial court at the time of framing of charge consider material filed by the accused, is the point for determination in these matters." After considering the arguments advanced the Court concluded:

"If the contention of the accused is accepted, there would be a mini trial at the stage of framing of charge. That would defeat the object of the Code. It is well-settled that at the stage of framing of charge the defence of the accused cannot be put forth. The acceptance of the contention of the learned counsel for the accused would mean permitting the accused to adduce his defence at the stage of framing of charge and for examination thereof at that stage which is against the criminal jurisprudence."

"It is in this light that the provision about hearing the submissions of the accused as postulated by Section 227 is to be understood. It only means hearing the submissions of the accused on the record of the case as filed by the prosecution and documents submitted therewith and nothing more. The expression 'hearing the submissions of the accused' cannot mean opportunity

to file material to be granted to the accused and thereby changing the settled law. At the state of framing of charge hearing the submissions of the accused has to be confined to the material produced by the police."

"As a result of aforesaid discussion, in our view, clearly the law is that at the time of framing charge or taking cognizance the accused has no right to produce any material. Satish Mehra's case holding that the trial court has powers to consider even materials which the accused may produce at the stage of Section 227 of the Code has not been correctly decided."

In Debendra Nath Padhi, the Court had relied on an earlier judgment in State, ACB Hyderabad vs. P. Suryaprakasam, 1999 SCC (Cri) 373, where a two judge bench of the Supreme Court had squarely considered the question of considering the material produced by the accused at the stage of framing of charge. The court held: *"According to the above sections, at the time of framing of a charge what the trial court is required to, and can, consider are only the police report referred to under section 173 CrPC and the documents sent with it. The only right the accused has at that stage is of being heard and nothing beyond that. **Of, course, at that stage the accused may be examined but that is prerogative of the court only....**"* (emphasis supplied).

On the question of scrutinizing material sent with a report under section 173 CrPC, there is no doubt that such material has to be scrutinized before framing charges. But in Debendra Nath Padhi, the court did make some further observations on the requirements for framing of charge which may create a doubt whether the observations in Satish Mehra, that if a case is to certainly end in acquittal, accused may not be made to undergo ordeal of a trial, too has been disapproved. The observations are as under:

" ... *The court may, for this limited purpose, sift the evidence as it cannot be expected even at that initial stage to accept all that the prosecution states as gospel truth even if it is opposed to common sense or the broad probabilities of the case.*

*All the decisions, when they hold that there can only be limited evaluation of materials and documents on record and **sifting of evidence** to prima facie find out whether sufficient ground exists or not for the purpose of proceeding further with the trial, **have so held with reference to materials and documents produced by the prosecution and not the accused**. .."* (emphasis supplied).

Though what is suggested is that if it is a balancing case still a charge may be framed, this does not affect the observations in Satish Mehra that when "Judge is fairly certain that there is no prospect of the case ending in conviction" i.e. when the case is not balancing, but when the scales have totally tilted in favour of a certain acquittal, the judge may not frame charge. Let us not confuse the expression **"At that stage, the court is not to see whether there is sufficient ground for conviction of the accused or whether the trial is sure to end in his conviction"** as contradicting what was held in Satish Mehra. At the cost of repetition it has to be pointed out that in Satish Mehra, the court exhorts that when there is a certainty that the case is to end in acquittal, there is no point in putting the accused to trial. The gap between certainty of conviction and certainty of acquittal may be perceived.

In fact, the focus in Debendra Nath Padhi was on finding if a criminal court could look into material produced by the accused at the stage of framing of charge. And on that issue the Court is clear that material produced by the accused cannot be looked into. So, Satish Mehra was overruled only to that extent. It would be wrong to conclude that the observations in Satish Mehra that *"But when the Judge is fairly certain that there is no prospect of the case ending in conviction the valuable time of the Court should not be wasted for holding a trial only for the purpose of formally completing the procedure to pronounce the conclusion on a future date. We are under heavy pressure of work-load.",* have been disapproved. So, if not the high standard laid down in Century Mills, which it is humbly submitted, is the only correct reading of provisions about framing of charge, there can be no excuse for not following the lesser requirement laid down in Satish Mehra that when the judge is fairly certain that there is no prospect of case ending in conviction, the accused should not be charged and should not be put to trial. One can find umpteen number of judgments where while justifying invocation of powers under section 482 of the Code for quashing prosecutions, the Courts have observed that putting a person through the grill of a criminal prosecution is a serious matter. In any case since, as pointed out earlier the provisions of the Code about requirements for framing charge in the three types of trials are unambiguous and do not call for any interpretation other than that a charge can be framed only if there is ground for presuming that the accused has committed an offence, as is held in Century Spg. and Mfg. co.

The question, whether accused could be examined at the stage when technically no 'evidence' as popularly understood is before the court, came up before a five judge bench of the Supreme court in AIR 1964 SUPREME COURT 949 "Ramnarayan Mor v. State of Maharashtra". It was a case under the old CrPC, when at the stage of committal, the magistrate was expected to record evidence. In that case, the Public Prosecutor submitted that since the evidence in that case was mainly documentary, the prosecution did not want to examine any witness at that stage, but wanted that the accused be examined. The magistrate granted this application and revision by the accused against this order was rejected by the High court. The accused approached the Supreme Court by filing a special leave petition. In the Supreme Court on some aspects, the court was divided. Three judges forming majority, were Chief Justice Sinha, Shah and Subba Rao. Speaking for the majority, Justice Shah noted the question raised by the accused as under: *"The appellants say that in enquiry for commitment to the Court of Session the accused person can be asked to explain circumstances appearing against him only from the oral evidence recorded under S. 207-A (4), and not from circumstances appearing from the documents furnished under S. 173(4) of the Code."*

The Court then observed in Para 6 *".:The Magistrate is also authorised to examine the accused if necessary, for the purpose of enabling him to explain any circumstances in the evidence against him. **The power is in terms discretionary-that is made clear by the use of the expression "if necessary" - but the discretion must be exercised on sound judicial principles having regard to the purpose of the inquiry which is to judicially ascertain whether there is a prima facie case made out against the accused for commitment.** ...It would indeed be surprising if the Legislature intended by using the expression "examine the*

62

accused for the purpose of enabling him to explain any circumstances appearing in the evidence against him" that the opportunity to be given to the accused for explaining circumstances appearing against him must be restricted to circumstances appearing from the oral evidence, whereas in making an order of commitment or discharge, the Magistrate may take into consideration the documents referred to in S. 173(4) as well as the oral evidence recorded in sub-s. (4) of section 207-A and afford an opportunity to the prosecutor and the accused of being heard on the entire record. Such a construction of the clause, by putting a restricted interpretation upon the cases, involves great prejudice to the accused. **The circumstance appearing against the accused would in a large majority of cases be from the statements recorded under S. 161 (3) under S. 164, and other documentary evidence but if the accused is not to be given an opportunity to explain those circumstances, to a large extent the judicial character of the proceeding would be impaired, for in determining whether the record discloses a prima facie case against the accused justifying an order of commitment to the Court of Session for trial, examination of the accused for the purpose of enabling him to explain any circumstances appearing against him only from the oral evidence and not from the documents referred to in S. 173(4) would fail to give to the Magistrate a complete picture of the** *case. The accused may have a complete answer to the documents on which the prosecution seeks to rely. ...*

...The object of the examination, it may be remembered, is to afford an opportunity to the accused to explain any circumstances appearing against him. He may avail himself of the opportunity, but he is not obliged to do so, and if he does not avail himself of the opportunity he is by the statute exposed to no prejudicial consequences." (emphasis supplied).

If the object of enabling a magistrate to examine the accused is understood properly, as explained in the observations quoted above, it would be clear that a magistrate may exercise discretion not to examine the accused only if the magistrate finds that there is no material for framing charges. If the magistrate is to put the accused to trial it would be incumbent on the magistrate to examine the accused, as the accused may have a complete answer to the material on which prosecution seeks to rely. Not doing so would amount to denying a valuable opportunity to the accused and making him go through the rigours of trial, as also heaping upon the court a needless trial. Unfortunately, courts routinely deny to the accused the opportunity to provide complete answer to the evidence sought to be tendered, if he has, and heap upon themselves needless trials. If the accused is examined at that stage with reference to not only documents sought to be tendered, but also to what witnesses are likely to state at trial from the statements recorded in course of investigation, the court may have a reliable explanation from the accused. In any case a substantial part of evidence at trial would be curtailed since the accused may not dispute a number of documents or facts. Since provisions of section 294 of the Code too are routinely overlooked, examination of the accused by the Court will save the Court a lot of valuable time lost in examining witnesses of a formal nature.

To sum up, it is imperative that the Supreme Court in an appropriate case reiterates that-

1. Magistrates must regularly call for and peruse case diaries in respect of all first information reports sent to the court, and ensure that the investigating officers promptly take all steps in investigation according to prescribed procedure and rules.

2. Magistrates must be fully trained to carefully scrutinise charge-sheets filed and issue process only if the charge-sheet prima facie discloses that there is material to proceed against the accused. This should be done even in cases triable by courts of sessions or special courts.

3. Magistrates must examine the accused with reference to material in the charge sheet before proceeding to frame charges.

4. Charges may be framed by sessions judges and magistrates only if the material on record, at its face value,

shows that there is ground to presume that the accused has committed the offence.

5. A criminal court must discharge the accused if it is certain that on the material tendered conviction is not possible.

6. All criminal courts must, in consultation with lawyers, fix programs for trials in such a manner that trials once begun end after day to day hearings and there is no occasion for adjournments.

7. Superior courts should as far as possible not interfere once a trial has begun and should not stay trials.

It is hoped that these steps may inject new life in the criminal justice system and mishaps like the one in case of gang rapes and murders from Nasik (Ankush Shinde case) or the Nithari killings do not recur. Let rule of law prevail.

5. Ignorance of law is no excuse for the common man, Ignoring law is qualification for reaching the top.

One could have ignored failure of justice in Ankush Shinde's case due to carelessness, or judgments glorifying deviation from prescribed procedures, or judgments ignoring settled precedent as aberrations. To err is human and judges are after all human beings. Rather, as former CJI Gogoi says, judges do not fall from heaven. But since these instances are not exceptions, and tend to grow in numbers they cannot be overlooked. I do not propose to bother readers with all such instances but point out glaring instances coming from those who reached the pinnacle.

CJI Sathasivam,albeit before he became CJI, (with Gogoi J who too became CJI), decided a case under the NDPS Act, reported in [2012] 10 S.C.R. 1157, SURESH & ORS. v. STATE OF MADHYA PRADESH. It was held on facts that: *"Para 2(b). ...During search, they found that each of the appellants was having a polythene bag in their possession which contained white colour substance and on its physical test, it was found "opium". The SDO (P), Radhogarh was informed about the incident. On weighing, all the three bags contained 825 gms, 820 gms and 800 gms of "Opium". Samples of 25 gms were taken separately from each of the packets and the contents were sealed. Thereafter, the* *vehicle was also searched and D inside the front mudguard, six packets of polythene bag containing 'opium' were also recovered weighing 810 gms, 820 gms, 690 gms, 820 gms, 800 gms and 615 gms respectively. Sample of 25 gms. from each of them were also taken and sealed. Thus, a total of 7 kg. Opium valued E at Rs.1,03,575/- was seized from the appellants and they were arrested.``*

After considering judgments on section 50 of the Act, the bench observed:

"12. We reiterate that subsection (1) of Section 50 makes it imperative for the empowered officer to "inform" the person concerned about the existence of his right that if he so requires, he shall be searched before a gazetted officer or a Magistrate, failure to do so vitiate the conviction and sentence of an accused where the conviction has been recorded only on the basis of possession of the contraband. We also reiterate that the said provision is mandatory and requires strict compliance.

*13. **Though a portion of the contraband (opium) was recovered from the vehicle for which Section 50 is not applicable, if we exclude the quantity recovered from the vehicle, the remaining would not come within the mischief of 'commercial quantity' for imposition of such conviction and sentence.** Taking note of length of period in prison and continuing as on date and in view of non-compliance of sub-section (1) of Section 50 in respect of* *recovery of contraband from the appellants, **we set aside the conviction** and sentence imposed on them by the trial Court and confirmed by the High Court.*

14. As a result, the appeal is allowed and the appellants G are ordered to be released forthwith, if they are not required in any other case." (emphasis supplied)

The judges may be right in excluding the quantity of contraband seized in personal searches because of violation of provisions of section 50. But what about the quantity seized from the car? The judges do not hold that this seizure is also tainted and to be ignored. Rather they curiously hold - *"**Though a portion of the contraband (opium) was recovered from the vehicle for which Section 50 is not applicable, if we exclude the quantity recovered from the vehicle, the remaining would not come within the mischief of 'commercial quantity' for imposition of such conviction and sentence."*** (emphasis supplied)

If the judges of the Supreme Court, both of whom later became Chief Justices of India, are so careless while delivering a judgment, as to exclude quantity recovered from the vehicle to which they say that section 50 is not applicable, how can common man expect careful scrutiny of cases from the highest court? This is not all. In all 7 kg of contraband was seized, out of which 2.445 kg (825 gms, 820 gms and 800 gms) was seized from personal searches. So the remaining quantity seized from the vehicle to which section 50 did not apply was 4.555kg (810 gms, 820 gms, 690 gms, 820 gms, 800 gms and 615 gms). Commercial quantity for opium is prescribed to be 2.5 kg. So how do judges hold that it was not a commercial quantity? Again this is not all. They, being weak in Mathematics, may be pardoned for concluding that it was not a commercial quantity. But even possession of non-commercial quantities is an offence, albeit attracting a lesser sentence. Then on what basis the Court held," **we set aside the conviction**". Did the court simply believe that this jugglery will not be noticed? This generosity in a case of huge quantity of drugs may be contrasted with six death sentences awarded in Ankush Shinde's case.

The bench was indeed generous for offenders caught with commercial quantities of drugs. In Shahejadkhan Mahebubkhan Pathan v. State of Gujarat, by P. SATHASIVAM AND RANJAN GOGOI, JJ., reported at [2012] 8 S.C.R. 1177, the bench was considering possession of 500 gms of brown sugar, which is commercial quantity. The Court held as to sentence, " *9. It is projected before us that both the appellants are first time offenders and there is no past antecedent about their involvement in offence of like nature on earlier occasions. It is further brought to our notice, which is also not disputed by the learned counsel for the State, that as on date, the appellants had served nearly 12 years in jail. In view of the same and in the light of the decision of this Court, in Balwinder Singh (supra), while confirming the conviction, we reduce the sentence to 10 years which is the minimum prescribed sentence under the relevant provisions of the NDPS Act.*

Default Sentence:

*10. Coming to the next claim of the appellants, i.e., default sentence, the trial Judge, taking note of various aspects including the fact that the **appellants were carrying commercial quantity of brown sugar from the State of Madhya Pradesh to the State of Gujarat for doing business,** imposed a fine of Rs.1.5 lakh each, in default, ordered to undergo RI for 3 years.*

....

13. While taking note of the above principles, we are conscious of the fact that the present case is under the NDPS Act and for certain offences, the Statute has provided minimum sentence as well as minimum fine amount. In the earlier part of our judgment, taking note of the fact that the appellants being the first time offenders, we imposed the minimum sentence, i.e.,10 years instead of 15 years as ordered by the trial Court. In other words, the appellants have been ordered to undergo substantive sentence of RI for 10 years which is minimum. However, considering the circumstances placed before us on behalf of the appellants-accused, viz., they are very poor and have to maintain their family, it was their first offence and if they fail to pay the amount of fine as per the order of the Additional Sessions Judge, they have to remain in jail for a period of 3 years in addition to the period of substantive sentence because of their inability to pay the fine, we are of the view that serious prejudice will be caused not only to them but also to their family members who are innocent. We are, therefore, of the view that ends of justice would be met if we order that in default of payment of fine of Rs.1.5 lakhs, the appellants shall undergo RI for 6 months instead of 3 years as ordered by the Additional Sessions Judge and confirmed by the High Court." (emphasis supplied)

So much compassion for smuggling commercial quantities of brown sugar for doing business is indeed a glaring example of justice tempered with mercy! Judges were certainly not oblivious to the fact that their judgments will be followed by courts below and have cascading effect!

The decline, nay, the precipitate fall, begins with the Apex Court itself, when you see the court dumping all canons of justice to do what judges want. Throwing law and procedure to the wind! All the tall talk of principles of natural justice, 'audi alteram partem', deciding only the issues raised, crumbled long ago in the Apex Court itself. A matter pertaining to pension payable to Justice Kuldeep Singh who was directly appointed to the Supreme Court from the Bar was before the Court. (Kuldeep Singh vs.

Union of India WP civil 410/2001 2002(3)SCR620 =(2002) 9 SCC 218 decided on 29.04.2002). There was no question of how High Court judges are appointed or what should be the ratio between Bar appointees and service judges, which was then 60:40. Pertinently, service judges or their representatives were neither parties to the matter, nor was any notice issued to them. It will be useful to quote the whole order:

"In this writ petition, the question which arises for consideration relates to pension which is payable to a Judge who retires from this Court after having been appointed directly from the Bar. Similar question also arises with regard to Bar appointees to the High Courts. Experience has shown that the Bar appointees especially, if they are appointed at the age of 50 years and above get lesser pension than the Service Judge appointees. It is to be seen that as far as the Constitution of India is concerned, it stipulates the manner of appointment of the Judges and provides what may be termed as the qualification required for their appointment. The Constitution contemplates appointment to the High Courts from amongst members of the Bar as well as from amongst the Judicial Officers. The Constitution does not provide for any specific quota. Till a few years ago in practice 66-2/3% of vacancies were filled from amongst members of the Bar and 33-1-1/3% from the Judicial Services. It is only in the Conference of 4th December, 1993, of the Chief Ministers and the Chief Justices

that it was decided that the number of vacancies from amongst the judicial Officers "might go up to 40%." The decision of 4th December, 1993, cannot mean that the number of Judges from the Services have to be 40%. The normal practice which has been followed was 2/3rd and 1/3rd from amongst members of the Bar and Judicial Services respectively and it is only on a rare occasion that the Chief Justice of a High Court can propose more service Judges being appointed if suitable members of the Bar are not available. But this cannot be more than 40% in any case. It may here also be noted that in the Chief Justices' Conference held in 1999 it was unanimously resolved that the quota should normally be 66-2/3% and 33-1/3% and it is on this basis the Government should determine the likely number of Bar Judges and then consider whether the High Court Judges who are appointed from amongst the members of the Bar should not be given the same weightage as is now sought to be given to the members of the Bar who are appointed to this Court as far as pension is concerned.

To come up for further orders after the ensuing summer vacation."

The Bench was headed by Chief Justice B.N.Kirpal and had Justice Arijit Pasayat (whose bench had sentenced all six accused in Ankush Shinde to death), with Justice H.K. Sema, as member, decided that the ratio should be changed to two thirds

Bar judges and one third service judges! They could not be said to be ignorant about a long standing decision on principles of natural justice.

In State Of Orissa vs Dr. (Miss) Binapani Dei & Ors reported at 1967 AIR 1269, 1967 SCR (2) 625, the Court held:

*"The rule that a party to whose prejudice an order is intended to be passed is entitled to a hearing applies to judicial tribunals and bodies of persons invested with authority to adjudicate upon matters involving civil consequences. It is one of the fundamental rules of our constitution setup that every citizen is protected against exercise of arbitrary authority by the State or its officers. Duty to act judicially would therefore arise from the very nature of the function intended to be performed; it need not be shown to be super-added. If there is power to decide and determine to the prejudice of a person, duty to act judicially is implicit in the exercise of such power. **If the tails of justice be ignored and an order to the prejudice of a person is made, the order is a nullity.** That is a basic concept of the rule of law and importance thereof transcends the significance of a decision in any particular case."*

What was the cause for this sudden judicial fiat without making persons to whose prejudice the order was passed parties? If there was already a resolution of Chief justices and Chief Ministers Conference in 1999, was it not followed till 2002? How could that issue be a part of order in a case relating to pension payable

75

to a direct appointee to the Supreme Court? Only appointments and vacancies at that time will throw light. How does any Chief Justice or any jurist justify this high handedness? I quote this instance as a glaring example of how the apex court has dealt with appointments to the High Court and how it has treated district judiciary. Minor and major instances of routine injustice to district judiciary are galore. Euphemistic magnanimity in calling these courts district judiciary instead of subordinate courts does not heal the hurt of always looking at trial courts with suspicion, not supporting them. If the foundation of the judicial edifice is itself weakened, how could it be strong enough to bear the onslaught of present-day unethical politics?

Did any subsequent bench find it necessary to overrule CJ Kirpal? No, because it suited everyone in pushing their own proteges in High Courts. And I am sure even collegium will meekly follow this uncalled for order, which in terms of order in Binapani Dei is a nullity. One cannot avoid recalling what Jonathan Swift said about precedent: *"It is a maxim among these lawyers, that whatever hath been done before may legally be done again: and therefore they take special care to record all the decisions formerly made against common justice and the general reason of mankind. These, under the name of precedents, they produce as authorities, to justify the most iniquitous opinions; and the judges never fail of decreeing accordingly."*

6. Scars and dimples on the face of the goddess of justice.

For the Oxbridge Harford group, the only scar seen on the face of the goddess of justice is ADM Jabalpur, even after it was removed by 'No Scar' cream of a constitution amendment. And the only dimple seen is the obiter dictum in Maneka Gandhi, forgetting that there was no issue to be decided and so the observations did not qualify to be ratio or have any precedential value. But there are other scars left because the whitewashers did an incomplete job, not applying 'Caesar's wife' standard, leaving some high and mighty live and die with a cloud of doubt. But I will focus on only five of these scars.

The first is Justice Karnan being sent to Tihar for contempt. When a high court judge was making unholy noise, he was first transferred, branded insane, and his work was withdrawn. All fine. But after doubting his sanity and without any certificate about his sanity from a reliable medical board, he was convicted of criminal contempt by a specially constituted bench of unusual strength -seven judges! "It is elementary, My dear Watson", as Sherlock Holmes would have said, 'if a person is insane, he cannot be tried till he is declared fit for trial. This even a magistrate would know.' Any common man with common sense would also know that no lunatic is likely to accept his lunacy, except to avoid punishment, and therefore if an insane person says that he is fine, his self-certification is of no value. And why a seven-judge bench (when it now transpires that 250 references to seven and nine judge benches are pending for decades)? What about equality before law? Why was he given this special treatment? Was it because a bench ordinarily dealing with contempt petitions was not to be trusted? Or, was it to ensure that the decision would not be altered by any subsequent bench, which would require nine judges?

The second scar is leaving Chief justice Mohit Shah's role in the Loya affair in doubt. If a court asks a wrong question, it is bound to come with a wrong answer. Two questions publicly raised in the matter were: Was late judge Loya pressured to decide the matter involving Shri Amit Shah in favour of the accused by, among others, Chief Justice Shri Mohit Shah? The second was about how Shri Loya met with his death. If there were doubts about Shri Loya's death, because otherwise there would have been no occasion to have a post mortem examination conducted, that was clearly a matter for police to investigate and file an appropriate report before a magistrate. The Supreme Court could simply have told the petitioner to approach the police or a magistrate and allowed the law to take its course. But the Court took up the issue to put an end to speculations.[18] (The Court wonders why people have to approach it for small issues like bail.

The answer is 'because you entertain'.) If the Court did want to end all speculations, and indeed what ought to be the Court's main concern- the reputation of a Chief justice of a prominent High Court, it should have gone into that question and cleared the air, rather than making Chief Justice Shah live in a shadow of doubt about his involvement.

The third is CJI Ranjan Gogoi's holding a sitting of the Supreme Court in respect of allegations made by a female staffer. The Chief Justice of India who post-retirement proclaimed that courts did not deliver justice, convened the court on a non-working day. His version of the events from his autobiography, 'Justice for Judge', chapter 10 'SUPREME' ALLEGATIONS AND MY

QUEST FOR TRUTH is as under:

"Later that Friday night, I received information that an Article 32 petition was likely to be filed in the Supreme Court the next day i.e. 20 April, a Saturday, seeking, inter alia, orders restraining the CJI from discharging his duties until he was cleared of the allegations levelled by the staffer. **Obviously, the plan was to stop me, with immediate effect, from attending to any administrative or judicial work.** *The following morning, I rang up the Attorney General, the Solicitor General and the president of the SCBA to inform them of the developments. The Solicitor General requested that a Bench be constituted to decide whether judicial orders, if*

any, should be passed in the circumstances. **I reflected upon the matter and soon concluded that aggression would be the best form of defence in the circumstances.** I had no options.

I, therefore, informed the Registry and all concerned that there would be a special sitting of the Court consisting of Justice Arun Mishra, Justice Sanjiv Khanna and me at 10.30 a.m. Accordingly, the Bench assembled in Court No. 1. The Attorney General, the Solicitor General, the president of the SCBA and a few lawyers who were present were informed of the details of the allegations and the antecedents of the staffer, as revealed by her service record. This unscheduled hearing on Saturday which has been much talked about, was extremely short. **In fact, there was no hearing at all. I expressed my indignation at the allegations and maintained that it was an attempt by certain unknown quarters to jeopardize the functioning of the CJI.** At the end of the hearing, a very innocuous order was passed: ...

...

PRESUMED GUILTY?

... The lady staffer, who had brought the allegations, has been reinstated in service. She was dismissed from service sometime in December 2018 after an ex parte departmental proceeding in respect of certain specific charges which were in no way connected with the allegations levelled by her. The reinstatement was during my tenure as the CJI and not after my retirement, as *many believe or want believed because the reinstatement was made by Justice Bobde. It is little known that the reinstatement by Justice Bobde was made on humanitarian grounds, following the below petition submitted by the staffer to him on 1 November. He proceeded in the matter only after placing the petition before me and after I had passed orders requesting him to deal with the matter according to his discretion.*

To,

HMJ S.A. Bobde,

Hon'ble the Chief Justice of India designate, ...

Dated: 1-11-19

Sir,

With due respect, the applicant humbly pray to Your Lordship to reconsider the penalty of dismissal from service with effect from 21st December, 2018 as the applicant is finding extreme difficulty in finding a job and is facing hardship in the absence of employment.

This great institution has given me so much and an opportunity to learn for which I am grateful.

It is humbly prayed to Your Lordship to reconsider/review the order of punishment so that the undersigned can get employment and also to get relieved from the present state of hardship and financial stringencies.

Yours faithfully,

Sd/-

Views were also expressed that as the staffer had been reinstated subsequent to my retirement, the allegations must have been legitimate. This conclusion is wrongly drawn because the staffer's petition for reinstatement was filed on 1 November; I passed orders on 5 November, requesting Justice Bobde to take a decision in the matter. I understand that, pursuant to Justice Bobde's orders, consequential reinstatement orders were passed on 7 November and she rejoined duties on 13 November—all the dates were within my tenure. Could there have been anything in exchange, as alleged by certain other quarters? Obviously not. First of all, I had nothing to do with the reinstatement. The decision was taken by Justice Bobde. In any case, nothing was left for the CJI to gain; the damage had occurred much earlier. All that should not have been done had been done much earlier. The reinstatement made seven months after the closure of the inquiry could not logically have been the outcome of any quid pro quo, as many argued.

Compassion is an integral part of administrative decision-making. ..." (emphasis supplied)

It was indeed bold of the former CJI to state facts in his autobiography. From what he recounts, following facts emerge:

a. There were some charges against the lady staffer as a result of which after an *ex-parte* departmental enquiry she was dismissed

82

from service on 21st December 2018. (It would have been useful if the charges for which she was dismissed were also stated, to gauge their gravity.)

b. On the 19th April, 2019 the CJI received information (must be obviously reliable information and not gossip or rumours) that on the next day a petition under article 32 was to be filed, and as the CJI states, '**Obviously, the plan was to stop me, with immediate effect, from attending to any administrative or judicial work.**'

c. The CJI thought, '**I reflected upon the matter and soon concluded that aggression would be the best form of defence in the circumstances.**'

d. On the 20th April,2019 '**In fact, there was no hearing at all. I expressed my indignation at the allegations and maintained that it was an attempt by certain unknown quarters to jeopardize the functioning of the CJI.**'

e. On 1-11-19 the staffer applied for reconsidering her punishment as she was suffering from financial hardship. There is no admission of guilt, no remorse, no apology in her letter.

f. She was reinstated and joined her services on the 13th November, 2019, very much during the tenure of Justice Gogoi.

g. Rather after she made allegations of sexual harassment for the sinister purpose of jeopardizing functioning of the CJI, she was shown compassion and reinstated, again without any apology or remorse for making scurrilous allegations in attempt to jeopardize the functioning of CJI. The allegations were made not to cause personal hurt to Justice Gogoi but to subvert the judicial process. No action of any kind was initiated against the staffer for levelling scurrilous allegations of sexual harassment against the CJI and no attempt to bring to expose and book those who tried to jeopardize the functioning of the CJI was made.

What is understood by an ignorant person like me is that the CJI had a whiff of a plan of a petition under article 32 being filed the next day and so he summoned the court on the next day after he '**concluded that aggression would be the best form of defence in the circumstances.**' It is not clear why the CJI should have been apprehensive about the petition under article 32. After all, it could not have been listed without his approval. So he need not have taken the unprecedented step of summoning the court. He was the CJI and is an honourable parliamentarian and has written the autobiography after the whole episode was over, obviously with due reflection, choosing words carefully (unlike my hasty expression). Therefore, when he says that aggression was the best defence, he places himself in the position of a person defending himself. Against what? Even if a petition was indeed filed, if it was the institution under attack, the institution would have taken care. Personally, Shri Gogoi had every right to show compassion and pardon the person for hurting him. It is laudable that our judges are like trees laden with fruit. If you pelt a stone of a slur on personal character, they reward with a fruit of reinstatement in service. But then does raising the personal slur to the level of attack on the institution, summoning a sitting of the Supreme Court of India to which the legal fraternity across the world looks up to for guidance, not reflect immaturity and impulsiveness? They are certainly not characters ideally associated with judges. This may be an example of how a judge commits contempt of his own court. When the institution was attacked, and a note of the attack was taken in a judicial proceeding before the highest court of the land, this ought to have been taken to its logical end.

Allegations by the staffer in order to jeopardize functioning of the office of CJI left a scar on the face of the goddess of justice, and unfortunately the account furnished by Justice Gogoi amounts to covering the scar with a bandage, making it more prominently noticeable.

The fourth is Justice Anand Vyankatesh's expose of the role of Madras high Court administration in transferring a case of a tainted politician at the final stage. Since this issue is far too fresh, it need not be elaborated. That the High Court administration could administratively transfer a sensitive matter to another officer and that officer should promptly come up with a clean chit for a politician, and that an anguished Justice Anand

Vyankatesh should take up the matter *suo moto* in revision and reverse the acquittal, show that the rot is far deeper than common man can perceive.

There is an advocate practising in the Madras High Court, who has written a book titled, "Courtroom wit and wisdom" wherein he recounts a story titled "Influential Justice", about a judge of Madras High Court being pressured by a Supreme Court judge to give a particular verdict and the high court judge succumbing to the pressure. Some years ago, late Dr Justice Lakshmanan was in tears in the court hall complaining that he was being pressured. Now if a judge of the Supreme Court is helpless and cannot sternly deal with such situations, how do we inspire trial courts without any protection to work without fear or favour?

Justice Raveendran notes, *"When there are murmurs about lack of integrity. Judiciary should maintain a constant vigil to ensure that corruption in any form does not enter its halls and corridors.*

There are different views on the question whether corruption in the judiciary should be discussed and dealt with. One view is that instances of corruption should be considered as mere aberrations and there should (not) be open debate as that tends to erode the confidence in the judiciary. It is pointed out that the trust and confidence will continue only if the judiciary is seen as a noble, virtuous and incorruptible institution; and if there is a constant talk or debate about corruption in the judiciary, even when the corruption is negligible, people will lose their faith in the judiciary, thereby eroding the strength of the judiciary."[19] It is submitted that rather than avoiding debate, this cancer needs to be dealt with sternly, before it spreads to the whole body.

And the last is the discovery by CJ Diwakar that the judge dealing with the Gyanvapi mosque case was hearing it without jurisdiction for two long years. Allahabad High Court Chief Justice Pritinker Diwaker has withdrawn cases related to the Kashi Vishwanath-Gyanvapi dispute from a single-judge bench of the High Court "in the interest of judicial propriety and judicial discipline as well as the transparency in the listing of cases".

In an order dated August 28,2023 Chief Justice Diwaker cited an order he passed on the administrative side on August 11, 2023 to "withdraw" the cases from the bench (of Justice Prakash Padia) "wherein the judgment is reserved and to nominate afresh".

In the order, the CJ notes: *"Record reveals that the cases were heard on 18.01.2021 by the Court which had the jurisdiction as per the roster assigned by the Chief Justice. After the cases were heard on several dates, the proceedings were concluded and judgment was reserved in the matter on 15.03.2021. The*

19   NJA journal p.100

judgment, however, was not delivered in the matter. The cases nevertheless continued to be listed before the same court even after the concerned learned Single Judge ceased to have jurisdiction in the matter as per roster."

"Facts of this case pose a more troubled scenario of procedural aberration. The non-observance of procedure in listing of the cases, passing of successive orders for reserving the judgment and again listing the cases before the learned Judge for hearing, though he no longer had jurisdiction in the matter as per the roster, under the directions received from the chamber of learned Judge, without allowing the parent section in the office to have access to the records of these cases are instances of non-observance of procedure settled for listing and hearing of cases," the order noted.

Now a judge of the High Court, who was not ignorant of the law of listing and roster, ignored for over two years that he ceased to have jurisdiction in the matter and proceeded to order the records to be produced before him. Two years were lost and now a fresh beginning will be made. How does it augur for the system plagued with vacancies and backlogs?

How do such persons enter the judiciary and climb to high positions? Is there something seriously wrong with our human resource management? In fact in "More Cries in wilderness" I had written, 'What is wrong with Court Management? Almost

Everything!'[20] People without a basic sense of justice enter judiciary and climb up the ladder, with cheerleaders clapping all along as they go on trampling upon law after law. Therefore....

20   More Cries in wilderness p.25.

7. Collegium and Memorandum of Procedure

Rule of law - 'Raj son of Kanoon', who escaped burial and ran away can be revived and lured back to the court if and only if we look at how we select judges. Apart from the examples in the preceding pages, when the Supreme Court berated two judges of different High Courts at different points of time for writing incomprehensible judgments, one wonders how the selectors had not noticed this lack of clarity when they were elevated, for they were elevated from judicial service and not from the Bar. Their judgments must have been scrutinised. If their judgments were intelligible and intelligent then, did they suddenly start writing incomprehensible prose? Or, is it you show me the dog and I will show you the rule?

I am not referring to failure of rule of precedent leading to deluge of cases pointed out by Barry Walsh[21], or the Nick Robinson[22] reports. Those interested may read them. They show that all is not well, rather nothing is well. One cannot help laughing when the Apex Court is anguished at people being required to approach it for seeking bail. Rather than finding out

21   Barry Walsh, International Journal For Court Administration | January 2008, p.23

22   Nick Robinson A Quantitative Analysis of the Indian Supreme Court's Workload (December 13, 2012). Journal of Empirical Legal Studies (Forthcoming),

causes for this situation, attempting systemic solutions, the powers that be go for quick fixes. They indulge in berating courts below, not realising that if courts below are manned by incompetent, inefficient spineless individuals, not steeped in sense of justice, they alone are responsible for this situation. They have the monopoly in appointing judges to constitutional courts, who in turn are charged with supervision and superintendence over district and trial courts. They control recruitment, training, and performance assessment as well as career growth. Justice S.B.Sinha in his public law lecture published in the NJA journal[23] has questioned if on the administrative side the High Courts have replaced rule of man (which now prevails) with rule of law? The answer will be an emphatic 'NO'.

If a correction has to be immediately applied, it ought to be in the selection of judges. Collegium was condemned by the Supreme Court too in the NJAC judgment, but neither the Union Government nor the Supreme Court came up with a new memorandum of procedure, possibly because it is easier to poke holes in others' creations. Or, is it that all parties are happy with the present give and take?

Since none of those responsible for taking up drafting of a new memorandum of procedure, let me outline some ideas which could in the interregnum be tested. This is what I suggest.

---

23   Justice Sinha NJA Journal p.77

- On the 1st June and 1st December every year let every High Court find vacancies for the high Court as well as all trial courts and tribunals. Existing vacancies as well as vacancies to occur in the next six months should be added. Broad categories from which these vacancies have to be filled may be identified and numbers to be filled in from these categories should be fixed (leaving out of course the coveted seat on the Bench for a community whose contribution in growth of law is said to be legendary).

- Examine all pendency and pattern of institution as well as disposal figures, and backlogs to identify areas of litigation which may be relevant while scouting talent.

- Simultaneously, check with reference to available databases the performance of existing manpower (expertise of judges) to meet the requirement and identify the shortfall for each category of litigation.

- Decide on zone of consideration or the catchment area by applying objective standards, like numbers available in pool, their length of practice where relevant, lower and outer limits, desired age groups to ensure long term availability, healthy competition, possibilities and necessity of limiting zone of consideration by number of years of practice.

- Announce the results of these steps so that persons in the zones can evaluate options. Those in the zones who may inform that they are not desirous of being considered may be excluded.

- From available databases, gather details of qualifications, experience, appearances, etc. in respect of persons in the zone. Analyse progress of cases in which each of these persons appeared. Examine judgments in those cases to find out if they possess requisite qualities like sense of justice, patience, expression, comprehension, communication skills, leadership qualities, ability to see beyond the facts of the case at hand etc.

- Instances of obstructionism, clashes with stakeholders, participation in boycotts and strikes may be identified.

- Since the records of all courts are digitized, examine pleadings and judgments digitally using AI tools, in cases conducted by the person concerned to find out if any flashes of excellence or undesirable aberrations are noticed. Wherever available, examine video recordings of court proceedings in which the persons shortlisted appeared.

- Communicate results of this scrutiny to the persons concerned should they so desire, so that mistakes in the scrutiny if any can be identified and eliminated.

- While selecting persons to be recommended for judgeships in the High Courts, identify from the available pool persons whose talents will be specially needed for filling up deficiencies in the available talent pool. Also identify persons on the basis of their age to have a good mix of those who will have different terms to ensure coherence and avoid unhealthy competition and leg pulling.

- Just as minutes of collegium meetings are put on the web site, put all the information which has gone into the process of recommendations on the website. CJI Chandrachud has not only opened up judgment databases and case histories, but is also vigorously pushing for live streaming of court proceedings. So at least let the data which has gone into decision making be made public.

- In order to validate key performance indices that would weigh in the selection process, we may check the data in respect of those who are actually working as judges presently by collecting similar data of their days in practice, just before their elevation.

The entire information may be shared with all the judges of the High Court as also with the Government. Their views too may be included while making recommendations. When this exercise is undertaken for the first time, data collection and analysis may take time. But thereafter only incremental data for six months will have to be added and analysed, which IT experts may facilitate. Only then will the judiciary show that there is no nepotism in the selection process. This will enhance public confidence in the system.

My punch may hurt. In fact, delivering it hurts me more than those inert bigwigs who are interested in visible reforms hogging publicity -as a bigwig called, plucking low hanging fruits, to show that they are doing something. They have reduced the judicial system to a safety valve in a turbulent society, more for the safety of the political class than the common man. Unlike "Yes My Lord, It's You in the Mirror," where I had tendered an advance apology, no apology or regrets this time.

***

You My lords,killed the rule of law. Now you have to take steps to resuscitate rule of law, breathe new vigour, hope of life to make the system relevant.

www.ingramcontent.com/pod-product-compliance
Lightning Source LLC
Chambersburg PA
CBHW062351290526
45794CB00005B/2179